FORWARD/COMMENTARY

The National Institute of Standards and Technology (NIST) is a measurement standards laboratory, and a non-regulatory agency of the **United States Department of Commerce**. Its mission is to promote innovation and industrial competitiveness. Founded in 1901, as the National Bureau of Standards, NIST was formed with the mandate to provide standard weights and measures, and to serve as the national physical laboratory for the United States. **With a** world-class measurement and testing laboratory encompassing a wide range of areas of computer science, mathematics, statistics, and systems engineering, NIST's cybersecurity program supports its overall mission to promote U.S. innovation and industrial competitiveness by advancing measurement science, standards, and related technology through research and development in ways that enhance economic security and improve our quality of life.

The need for cybersecurity standards and best practices that address interoperability, usability and privacy has been shown to be critical for the nation. NIST's cybersecurity programs seek to enable greater development and application of practical, innovative security technologies and methodologies that enhance the country's ability to address current and future computer and information security challenges.

The cybersecurity publications produced by NIST cover a wide range of cybersecurity concepts that are carefully designed to work together to produce a holistic approach to cybersecurity primarily for government agencies and constitute the best practices used by industry. This holistic strategy to cybersecurity covers the gamut of security subjects from development of secure encryption standards for communication and storage of information while at rest to how best to recover from a cyber-attack.

Why buy a book you can download for free?

Some are available only in electronic media. Some online docs are missing pages or barely legible.

We at 4th Watch Books are former government employees, so we know how government employees actually use the standards. When a new standard is released, an engineer prints it out, punches holes and puts it in a 3-ring binder. While this is not a big deal for a 5 or 10-page document, many NIST documents are over 100 pages and printing a large document is a time-consuming effort. So, an engineer that's paid $75 an hour is spending hours simply printing out the tools needed to do the job. That's time that could be better spent doing engineering. We publish these documents so engineers can focus on what they were hired to do – engineering. It's much more cost-effective to just order the latest version from Amazon.com

If there is a standard you would like published, let us know. Our web site is Cybah.webplus.net

Please see the Cybersecurity Standards list at the end of this book.

CyberSecurity Standards Library™

Get a Complete Library of Over 300 Cybersecurity Standards on 1 Convenient DVD!

The **4th Watch CyberSecurity Standards Library** is a DVD disc that puts over 300 current and archived cybersecurity standards from NIST, DOD, DHS, CNSS and NERC at your fingertips! Many of these cybersecurity standards are hard to find and we included the current version and a previous version for many of them. The DVD includes four books written by Luis Ayala: **The Cyber Dictionary, Cybersecurity Standards, Cyber-Security Glossary of Building Hacks and Cyber-Attacks**, and **Cyber-Physical Attack Defenses: Preventing Damage to Buildings and Utilities**.

- ✓ DVD includes many Hard-to-find Cybersecurity Standards - some still in Draft.
- ✓ Docs are organized by source and listed numerically so each standard is easy to locate.
- ✓ The listing of standards on the DVD includes an abstract of the subject, and date issued.
- ✓ PDF format for use on PC, Mac, eReaders, or tablets.
- ✓ No need for WiFi / Internet.
- ✓ Save countless hours of searching and downloading.
- ✓ Carry in a briefcase - terrific for travel.

4th Watch Publishing is releasing the CyberSecurity Standards Library DVD to make it easier for you to access the tools you need to ensure the security of your computer networks and SCADA systems. We also publish many of these standards on demand so you don't need to waste valuable time searching for the latest version of a standard, printing hundreds of pages and punching holes so they can go in a three-ring binder. **Order on Amazon.com**

The DVD works on PC and Mac with the standards in PDF format. To view the CyberSecurity Standards Library on the DVD, a computer with a DVD drive is required. The most current version of your internet browser, at least 2GB of RAM, and current version of Adobe Reader is recommended. (Compatible browsers include Internet Explorer 8+, Mozilla Firefox 4+, Apple Safari 5+, Google Chrome 15+)

National Institute of Standards and Technology

U.S. Department of Commerce

NIST Interagency Report 7788

Security Risk Analysis of Enterprise Networks Using Probabilistic Attack Graphs

Anoop Singhal
Ximming Ou

NIST Interagency Report 7788

Security Risk Analysis of Enterprise
Networks Using Probabilistic Attack
Graphs

Anoop Singhal
Ximming Ou

C O M P U T E R   S E C U R I T Y

Computer Security Division
Information Technology Laboratory
National Institute of Standards and Technology
Gaithersburg, MD 20899-8930

August 2011

U.S. Department of Commerce

Rebecca M. Blank, Acting Secretary

National Institute of Standards and Technology

Patrick D. Gallagher, Director

Reports on Computer Systems Technology

The Information Technology Laboratory (ITL) at the National Institute of Standards and Technology (NIST) promotes the U.S. economy and public welfare by providing technical leadership for the nation's measurement and standards infrastructure. ITL develops tests, test methods, reference data, proof of concept implementations, and technical analysis to advance the development and productive use of information technology. ITL's responsibilities include the development of technical, physical, administrative, and management standards and guidelines for the cost-effective security and privacy of sensitive unclassified information in federal computer systems. This Internal Report discusses ITL's research, guidance, and outreach efforts in computer security and its collaborative activities with industry, government, and academic organizations.

National Institute of Standards and Technology Interagency Report 7788
 # pages (August 2011)

Acknowledgements

The authors Anoop Singhal and Ximming Ou would like to thank their colleagues who reviewed drafts of this document and contributed to its development. A special note of thanks goes to Peter Mell, Harold Booth, Ron Boisvert, Ramaswamy Chandramouli, and Kevin Stine of NIST for serving as reviewers for this document. The authors also acknowledge Elizabeth Lennon for her technical editing and administrative support.

Executive Summary

Today's information systems face sophisticated attackers who combine multiple vulnerabilities to penetrate networks with devastating impact. The overall security of an enterprise network cannot be determined by simply counting the number of vulnerabilities. To more accurately assess the security of enterprise systems, one must understand how vulnerabilities can be combined and exploited to stage an attack. Composition of vulnerabilities can be modeled using probabilistic attack graphs, which show all paths of attacks that allow incremental network penetration. Attack likelihoods are propagated through the attack graph, yielding a novel way to measure the security risk of enterprise systems. This metric for risk mitigation analysis is used to maximize the security of enterprise systems. This methodology based on probabilistic attack graphs can be used to evaluate and strengthen the overall security of enterprise networks.

Audience

This document is intended for three primary audiences:

- Federal agencies seeking information on how to use probabilistic attack graphs for security risk analysis of their enterprise networks;

- Vendor communities seeking to understand the methodology of security risk analysis using probabilistic attack graphs and to build new tools in this area; and

- Research communities seeking to understand some of the challenges in the area of enterprise network security and new research opportunities to address problems in this area.

Table of Contents

1. Introduction

At present, computer networks constitute the core component of information technology infrastructures in areas such as power grids, financial data systems, and emergency communication systems. Protection of these networks from malicious intrusions is critical to the economy and security of our nation. Vulnerabilities are regularly discovered in software applications which are exploited to stage cyber attacks. Currently, management of security risk of an enterprise network is more an art than a science. System administrators operate by instinct and experience rather than relying on objective metrics to guide and justify decision making. In this report, we develop models and metrics that can be used to objectively assess the security risk in an enterprise network, and techniques on how to use such metrics to guide decision making in cyber defense.

To improve the security of enterprise networks, it is necessary to measure the amount of security provided by different network configurations. The objective of our research was to develop a standard model for measuring security of computer networks. A standard model will enable us to answer questions such as "Are we more secure than yesterday?" or "How does the security of one network configuration compare with another?" Also, having a standard model to measure network security will bring together users, vendors, and researchers to evaluate methodologies and products for network security.

Some of the challenges for security risk analysis of enterprise networks are:

a) *Security vulnerabilities are rampant:* CERT[1] reports about a hundred new security vulnerabilities each week. It becomes difficult to manage the security of an enterprise network (with hundreds of hosts and different operating systems and applications on each host) in the presence of software vulnerabilities that can be exploited.

b) *Attackers launch complex multistep cyber attacks:* Cyber attackers can launch multistep and multi-host attacks that can incrementally penetrate the network with the goal of eventually compromising critical systems. It is a challenging task to protect the critical systems from such attacks.

c) *Current attack detection methods cannot deal with the complexity of attacks:* Computer systems are increasingly under attack. When new vulnerabilities are reported, attack programs are available in a short amount of time. Traditional approaches to detecting attacks (using an Intrusion Detection System) have problems such as too many false positives, limited scalability, and limits on detecting attacks.

Good metrics should be measured consistently, inexpensive to collect, expressed numerically, have units of measure, and have specific context [1]. We meet this challenge by capturing vulnerability interdependencies and measuring security in the exact way that real attackers penetrate the network. We analyze all attack paths through a network, providing a metric of overall system risk. Through this metric, we analyze trade-offs between security costs and security benefits. Decision makers can therefore avoid over investing in security measures that do not pay off, or under investing and risk devastating consequences. Our metric is consistent, unambiguous, and provides context for understanding security risk of computer networks.

This report is organized as follows. Section 2 presents attack graphs and tools for generating attack graphs. Section 3 discusses past work in the area of security risk analysis. Section 4 discusses the Common Vulnerability Scoring System (CVSS). Section 5 discusses security risk analysis of enterprise

---

[1] Computer Emergency Response Team, http://www.cert.org/

networks using attack graphs. Section 6 presents some of the challenges for security risk analysis and, finally, Section 7 gives the conclusions.

2. Attack Graphs

Attack graphs model how multiple vulnerabilities may be combined for an attack. They represent system states using a collection of security-related conditions, such as the existence of vulnerability on a particular host or the connectivity between different hosts. Vulnerability exploitation is modeled as a transition between system states.

As an example, consider Figure 1. The left side shows a network configuration, and the right side shows the attack graph for compromise of the database server by a malicious workstation user. In the network configuration, the firewall is intended to help protect the internal network. The internal file server offers file transfer (ftp), secure shell (ssh), and remote shell (rsh) services. The internal database server offers ftp and rsh services. The firewall allows ftp, ssh, and rsh traffic from a user workstation to both servers, and blocks all other traffic.

In the attack graph, attacker exploits are blue ovals, with edges for their preconditions and postconditions. The numbers inside parentheses denote source and destination hosts. Yellow boxes are initial network conditions, and the green triangle is the attacker's initial capability. Conditions induced by attacker exploits are plain text. The overall attack goal is a red octagon. The figure also shows the direct impact of blocking ssh or rsh traffic (to the fileserver) through the firewall, i.e., preventing certain exploits in the attack graph.

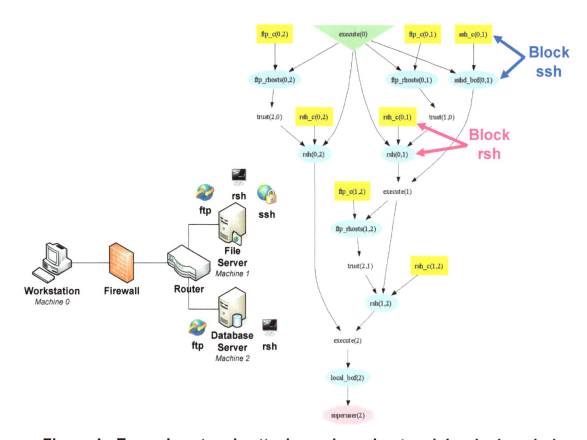

Figure 1: Example network, attack graph, and network hardening choices

The attack graph includes these attack paths:

a) *sshd_bof(0,1)* → *ftp_rhosts(1,2)* → *rsh(1,2)* → *local_bof(2)*
b) *ftp_rhosts(0,1)* → *rsh(0,1)* → *ftp_rhosts(1,2)* → *rsh(1,2)* → *local_bof(2)*
c) *ftp_rhosts(0,2)* → *rsh(0,2)* → *local_bof(2)*

The first attack path starts with *sshd_bof(0,1)*. This indicates a buffer overflow exploit executed from *Machine 0* (the workstation) against *Machine 1* (the file server), i.e., against its secure shell service. In a buffer overflow attack, a program is made to erroneously store data beyond a fixed-length buffer, overwriting adjacent memory that holds program control-flow data. The result of the *sshd_bof(0,1)* exploit is that the attacker can execute arbitrary code on the file server. The *ftp_rhosts(1,2)* exploit is now possible, meaning that the attacker exploits a particular ftp vulnerability to anonymously upload a list of trusted hosts from *Machine 1* (the file server) to *Machine 2* (the database server). The attacker can leverage this new trust to remotely execute shell commands on the database server, without providing a password, i.e., the *rsh(1,2)* exploit. This exploit establishes the attacker's control over the database server as a user with regular privileges. A local buffer overflow exploit is then possible on the database server, which runs in the context of a privileged process. The result is that the attacker can execute code on the database server with full privileges.

2.1 Tools for Generating Attack Graphs

This section describes briefly the tools available for generating attack graphs for enterprise networks.

- TVA (Topological Analysis of Network Attack Vulnerability)

  In [12] [13] [22], the authors describe a tool for generation of attack graphs. This approach assumes the monotonicity property of attacks, and it has polynomial time complexity. The central idea is to use an *exploit dependency graph* to represent the pre- and postconditions for an exploit. Then a graph search algorithm is used to chain the individual vulnerabilities and find attack paths that involve multiple vulnerabilities.

- NETSPA (A Network Security Planning Architecture)

  In [29] [30], the authors use attack graphs to model adversaries and the effect of simple counter measures. It creates a network model using firewall rules and network vulnerability scans. It then uses the model to compute network reachability and attack graphs representing potential attack paths for adversaries exploiting known vulnerabilities. This discovers all hosts that can be compromised by an attacker starting from one or more locations. NETSPA typically scales as $O(n\log n)$ as the number of hosts in a typical network increases. Risk is assessed for different adversaries by measuring the total assets that can be captured by an attacker.

- MULVAL (Multihost, multistage, Vulnerability Analysis)

  In [31] [32], a network security analyzer based on Datalog is described. The information in vulnerability databases, the configuration information for each machine, and other relevant information are all encoded as Datalog facts. The reasoning engine captures the interaction among various components in the network. The reasoning engine in MULVAL scales well ($O(n^2)$) with the size of the network.

  In [19] [20] [23] [24], some recent commercial tools for vulnerability analysis and attack graph generation are described. Skybox security [19] and Red Seal Systems [20] have developed a tool that can generate attack graphs. Risk is calculated using the probability of success of an attack path multiplied by the loss associated with the compromised target. Nessus [23] and Retina [24] are vulnerability management systems that can help organizations with vulnerability assessment, mitigation, and protection.

All the tools for attack graph generation that are mentioned here are similar in capabilities. We will use the MULVAL tool in this document to illustrate our methodology of security risk analysis using attack graphs.

3. Past Work in Security Risk Analysis

Modelers generally think about security in terms of threats, risks, and losses [1]. Good models provide a rationale for measurements, and these models can be updated and calibrated as new data becomes available. A data model can also be used to automate security calculations. Some of the benefits of automating security metrics calculations are:

- **Accuracy:** Accuracy is required to trust the data that is collected and to develop consensus about the results.
- **Repeatability:** This is another important component of trust. If two measurements of a target can give the same consistent result, then the data can be trusted.
- **Reliability:** Automation of data collection will result in more reliability as it is not prone to human errors.
- **Transparency:** The steps used to derive the metrics are readily apparent, and they are accurately documented.

Security metrics have been suggested based on criteria compliance, intrusion detection, security policy, security incidents, and actuarial modeling. Statistical methods (Markov modeling, Bayesian networks, etc.) have been used in measuring network security. Complementary to our approach, measurements of attack resistance [2] and weakest successful adversary [3] have been proposed.

Early standardization efforts in the defense community evolved into the system security engineering capability maturity model (SSE-CMM) [4], although it does not assign quantitative measures. Lots of risk management work has been done at the National Institute of Standards and Technology (NIST) on risk identification, assessment and analysis. NIST Special Publication (SP) 800-55 [5] describes the security metrics implementation process. NIST SP 800-27 [6] describes the principles for establishing a security baseline. NIST SP 800-39 [38] is the document that describes information security standards and guidelines developed by NIST. The purpose of NIST SP 800-39 is to provide a guide for an organization-wide program for managing information security risk. NIST SP 800-55 (Revision 1) [37] provides performance measurement guide for information security. NIST SP 800-30 [36] presents a risk management guide for information technology systems. There are also standardization efforts for vulnerability scoring, such as the Common Vulnerability Scoring System (CVSS) [7], although these treat vulnerabilities in isolation, without considering attack interdependencies on target networks.

In early work in attack graph analysis, model checking was used to enumerate attack sequences linking initial and goal states [8][9]. Because of explicit enumeration of attack states, these approaches scale exponentially with the size of the network. With a practical assumption of monotonic logic, attack graph complexity has been shown to be polynomial rather than exponential [10][11]. Graph complexity has been further reduced, to worst-case quadratic in the number of hosts [12].

Further improvement is possible by grouping networks into protection domains, in which there is unrestricted connectivity among hosts within each domain [13]. With this representation, complexity is reduced to linear within each protection domain, and overall quadratic in the number of protection domains (which is typically much less than the number of hosts). Such attack graphs have been generated for tens of thousands of hosts (hundreds of domains) within a minute, excluding graph visualization [12]. A detailed description of this approach to attack graph analysis is given in [13] [14] [15].

Beyond improving attack graph complexity, frameworks have been proposed for expressing network attack models [16] [17][18]. Capabilities for mapping multistep attacks have begun to appear in some commercial products [19] [20], although their limitations include not showing all possible attack paths simultaneously as needed for effective risk assessment. A more extensive review of attack graph research (as of 2005) is given in [21].

There have been some attempts at measuring network security risk by combining attack graphs with individual vulnerability metrics. Frigault et al. [27] proposes converting attack graphs and individual vulnerability score into Bayesian Network for computing the cumulative probability. Wang et al. [25] recognize the existence of cycles in an attack graph and present ideas about how to propagate probabilities over cycles. In [26], techniques for enterprise network security metrics are described. In [28] [33], the concept of "Measuring the Attack Surface" is used to determine the security risk of software systems. In [34], a practical approach to quantifying security risk in enterprise networks is described.

In this report, we identify two layers in enterprise network security metrics: the *component metrics* and the *cumulative metrics*. The component metrics are about individual components' properties, which in many cases can be obtained from standard data sources like the National Vulnerability Database (NVD). The important feature of the component metrics is that they are only about individual components and do not consider interactions among components. As a result, they can be measured or computed separately. The cumulative security metrics account for both the baseline metrics of individual components and the interactions among components. We propose that the cumulative metrics shall be obtained by composing the component metrics through a *sound theoretical model with well-defined semantics*.

4. Common Vulnerability Scoring System (CVSS)

CVSS [7] is an industry standard for assessing the **severity** of computer system security vulnerabilities. It attempts to establish a measure of how much concern a vulnerability warrants, compared to other vulnerabilities, so efforts can be prioritized. It offers the following benefits:

- *Standardized Vulnerability Scores*: When an organization normalizes vulnerability scores across all of its software and hardware platforms, it can leverage a single vulnerability management policy.
- *Open Framework*: Users can be confused when a vulnerability is assigned an arbitrary score. With CVSS, anyone can see the individual characteristics used to derive a score.
- *Prioritized Risk*: When the environmental score is computed, the vulnerability now becomes contextual. That is, vulnerability scores are now representative of the actual risk to an organization.

CVSS is composed of three metric groups: *Base*, *Temporal*, and *Environmental*, each consisting of a set of metrics, as shown in Figure 2.

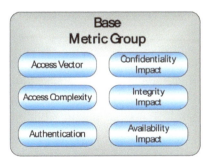  

Figure 2: CVSS Metric Groups

These metric groups are described as follows:

- *base*: representing "intrinsic and fundamental characteristics of a vulnerability that are constant over time and user environments"
- *temporal*: representing "characteristics of a vulnerability that change over time but not among user environments"
- *environmental*: representing "characteristics of a vulnerability that are relevant and unique to a particular user's environment"

The base metric group captures the characteristics of a vulnerability that do not change with time and across user environment. The Access Vector, Access Complexity, and Authentication metrics capture how the vulnerability is accessed and whether or not extra conditions are required to exploit it. The three impact metrics measure how a vulnerability, if exploited, will directly effect the degree of loss of confidentiality, integrity, and availability. For example, a vulnerability could cause a partial loss of integrity and availability, but no loss of confidentiality. We briefly describe the metrics as follows.

Access Vector (AV): This metric reflects how the vulnerability is exploited. The possible values for this metrics are: Local (L), Adjacent Network (A), and Network (N). The more remote an attacker can attack a host, the greater the vulnerability score.

Access Complexity (AC): This metric measures the complexity of the attack required to exploit the vulnerability once an attacker has gained access to the target system. The possible values for this metric are: High (H), Medium (M), and Low (L). For example, consider a buffer overflow in an Internet service. Once the target system is located, the attacker can launch and exploit it at will. The lower the required complexity, the higher the vulnerability score.

Authentication (AU): This metric measures the number of times an attacker must authenticate in order to exploit a vulnerability. This metric does not gauge the strength complexity of the authentication process, but only that an attacker is required to provide credentials before an exploit is launched. The possible values for this metric are: Multiple (M), Single (S), and None (N). The fewer authentication instances that are required, the higher the vulnerability scores.

Confidentiality Impact (C): This metric measures the impact on confidentiality of a successfully exploited vulnerability. Confidentiality refers to limiting information access and disclosure to only authorized users, as well as preventing access by, or disclosure to, unauthorized ones. The possible values for this metric are: None (N), Partial (P), and Complete (C). Increased confidentiality impact increases the vulnerability score.

Integrity Impact (I): This metric measures the impact to integrity of a successfully exploited vulnerability. Integrity refers to the trustworthiness and guaranteed veracity of information. The possible values for this metric are: None (N), Partial (P), and Complete (C). Increased integrity impact increases the vulnerability score.

Availability Impact (A): This metric measures the impact to availability caused by a successfully exploited vulnerability. Availability refers to the accessibility of information resources. Attacks that consume network bandwidth, processor cycles, or disk space all impact the availability of a system. The possible values for this metric are: None (N), Partial (P), and Complete (C). Increased availability impact increases the vulnerability score.

AN EXAMPLE

Consider CVE-2003-0062: Buffer Overflow in NOD32 Antivirus. NOD32 is an antivirus software application developed by Eset. In February 2003, a buffer overflow vulnerability was discovered in Linux and Unix versions prior to 1.013 that could allow local users to execute arbitrary code with the privileges of the user executing NOD32. To trigger the buffer overflow, the attacker must wait for (or coax) another user (possible root) to scan a directory path of excessive length.

Since the vulnerability is exploitable only to a user locally logged into the system, the Access Vector is "Local." The Access Complexity is "High" because this vulnerability can be exploited only under specialized access conditions. There is an additional layer of complexity because the attacker must wait for another user to run the virus-scanning software. Authentication is set to "None" because the attacker does not need to authenticate to any additional system. Together, these metrics produce a base score of 6.2.

The base vector for this vulnerability is :AV:L/AC:H/Au:N/C:C/I:C/A:C

		Base
Metric	Evaluation	Score
Access Vector	[Local]	(0.395)
Access Complexity	[High]	(0.35)
Authentication	[None]	(0.704)
Confidentiality Impact	[Complete]	(0.66)
Integrity Impact	[Complete]	(0.66)
Availability Impact	[Complete]	(0.66)
Formula		Base Score

Impact = 10.41 * (1 − (0.34 * 0.34 * 0.34)) = =10.0
Exploitability = 20 * 0.35 * 0.704 * 0.395 = = 1.9
f(Impact) = 1.176
Base Score = ((0.6*10) +(0.4*1.9)-1.5)*1.176 = 6.2

Basically, for each metric group, an equation is used to weigh the corresponding metrics and produce a score (ranged from 0 to 10) based on a series of measurements and security experts' assessment, and the score 10 represents the most severe vulnerability. Specifically, when the base metrics are assigned values, the base equation calculates a score ranging from 0 to 10, and creates a vector. This vector is a text string that contains the values assigned to each metric. It is used to communicate exactly how the score for each vulnerability is derived, so that anyone can understand how the score was derived and, if desired, confirm the validity of each metric.

Optionally, the base score can be refined by assigning values to the temporal and environmental metrics. This is useful in order to provide additional context for a vulnerability by more accurately reflecting the risk posed by the vulnerability to a user's environment. Depending on one's purpose, the base score and vector may be sufficient. If a temporal score is needed, the temporal equation will combine the temporal metrics with the base score to produce a temporal score ranging from 0 to 10. Similarly, if an environmental score is needed, the environmental equation will combine the environmental metrics with the base score to produce an environmental score ranging from 0 to 10. More details on base, temporal, and environmental equations, and the calculations can be found in the CVSS standards guide [8].

5. Security Risk Analysis of Enterprise Networks Using Attack Graphs

In this section, we present our methodology for security risk analysis of Enterprise Networks using Attack Graphs. We will use the MULVAL tool for attack graph generation to illustrate our approach. We explain our methodology using three examples. Example one presents the methodology using a single vulnerability. Examples two and three present the methodology for a system containing multiple vulnerabilities.

Attack graphs provide the cumulative effect of attack steps to show how each of these steps can potentially enable an attacker to reach their goal. However, one limitation of an attack graph is that it assumes that a vulnerability can always be exploited. In reality, there is a wide range of probabilities that different steps can be exploited. It is dependent on the skill of the attacker and the difficulty of the exploit. Attack graphs show what is possible without any indication of what is likely. In this section, we present a methodology to estimate the security risk using the CVSS scores of individual vulnerabilities.

Example 1

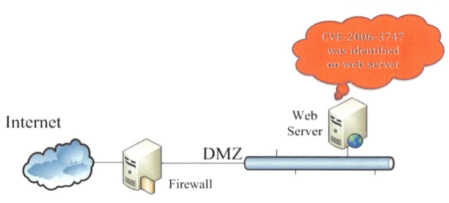

Figure 3

In the simple example of Figure 3, there is a firewall controlling network access from the Internet to the DMZ subnet of an enterprise network. The Demilitarized Zone (DMZ) is typically used to place publicly accessible servers, in this case the web server. The firewall protects the host in DMZ and only allows external access to ports necessary for the service. In this example, Internet is allowed to access the web server through TCP port 80, the standard HTTP protocol and port.

Suppose a vulnerability scan is performed on the web server, and a vulnerability is identified. The CVE ID of the discovered vulnerability is CVE-2006-3747. Using this ID as a key, one can query the National Vulnerability Database (NVD) and obtain a number of important properties of the vulnerability. Below is an excerpt from the information retrieved from NVD about CVE-2006-3747:

Overview
Off-by-one error in the ldap scheme handling in the Rewrite module (mod_rewrite) in Apache 1.3 from 1.3.28, 2.0.46 and other versions before 2.0.59, and 2.2, when RewriteEngine is enabled, allows remote attackers to cause a denial of service (application crash) and possibly execute arbitrary code via crafted URLs that are not properly handled using certain rewrite rules.

Impact
CVSS Severity (version 2.0):

CVSS v2 Base Score:7.6 (HIGH) (AV:N/AC:H/Au:N/C:C/I:C/A:C) (legend)
Impact Subscore: 10.0
Exploitability Subscore: 4.9
CVSS Version 2 Metrics:
Access Vector: Network exploitable
Access Complexity: High
Authentication: Not required to exploit
Impact Type: Provides administrator access, Allows complete confidentiality, integrity, and availability violation; Allows unauthorized disclosure of information; Allows disruption of service

The "Overview" section gives a number of key features of the vulnerability, including the relevant software modules and versions and what security impact the vulnerability poses to a system. The latter is further displayed in the "Impact" section. Most of the impact factors are expressed in the CVSS metric vector, which is "AV:N/AC:H/Au:N/C:C/I:C/A:C" in this case.

These CVSS metrics provide crucial information regarding the pre- and postconditions for exploiting the vulnerability. Such information can then be used to construct an attack graph, which shows all possible attack paths in a network. The attack graph for this simple network is shown in Figure 4.

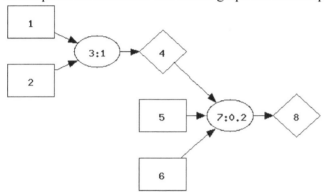

Figure 4

The meaning of the node labels are explained below:

1: hacl(internet,webServer,httpProtocol,httpPort)
2: attackerLocated(internet)
3: direct network access
4: netAccess(webServer,httpProtocol,httpPort)
5: networkServiceInfo(webServer,httpd,httpProtocol,httpPort,apache)
6: vulExists(webServer,'CVE-2006-3747',httpd,remote,privEscalation)
7: remote exploit of a server program
8: execCode(webServer,apache)

The above graph is computed from the MulVAL network security analyzer [31, 32]. The square vertices represent configuration of the system, e.g., the existence of a software vulnerability on a machine (node 6), firewall rules that allow Internet to access the web server through the HTTP protocol and port (node 1), and services running on a host (node 5). The diamond vertices represent potential privileges an attacker could gain in the system, e.g., code execution privilege on web server (node 8). The elliptical vertices are "attack nodes" which link preconditions to postconditions of an attack. For example, node 7 represents the attack "remote exploit of a server program." Its preconditions are: the attacker has network access to the target machine for the specific protocol and port (node 4), the service on that port is running (node 5), and the service is vulnerable (node 6). The postcondition of the attack is that the attacker gains the specific privilege on the machine (node 8).

An attack graph can help a system administrator understand what could happen in their network, through analyzing the configuration of an enterprise network system. When the size of the system increases, it becomes increasingly difficulty for a human to keep track of and correlate all relevant information. An automatic attack-graph generator has its unique advantage in that it can identify non-obvious attack possibilities arising from intricate security interactions within an enterprise network, which can be easily missed by a human analyst. It achieves this through building up a knowledge base (KB) about generic security knowledge independent of any specific scenarios. For example, the KB rule that generated part of the attack graph in Figure 4 is shown below.

```
execCode(H, Perm) :-
        vulExists(H, VulID, Software, remote, privEscalation),
        networkServiceInfo(H, Software, Protocol, Port, Perm),
        netAccess(H, Protocol, Port).
```

This is a generic Datalog rule for how to reason about remote exploit of a service program. It is easy to see that the three subgoals correspond to the three predecessors of node 7, and the head of the rule corresponds to its successor. The variables (in upper case-led identifiers) are automatically instantiated with the concrete values from a system's configuration tuples. There are many other rules like the one above in the knowledge base. All the rules form a Datalog program, and a Prolog system can efficiently evaluate such a program against thousands of input tuples. The evaluation process will find out *all* consequences arising from these rules. Complex multistep, multi-host attack paths are naturally captured in this logical reasoning process, even though each rule itself only describes a specific type of attack.

An attack graph is often perceived to have a deterministic semantics: as long as all the preconditions of an attack can be achieved, the attack can always succeed resulting in the attacker obtaining the postcondition privilege. In reality, it is often not that clear. The "possibly execute arbitrary code" in the vulnerability's overview highlights the uncertainty in the true consequence of exploiting a vulnerability. Depending on the difficulty level of the exploit, the attacker's skills and resources, and how hard it is to get to it, a vulnerability may or may not pose a high risk to the system. Since all security hardening measures (e.g., patching) inevitably incur cost in terms of human labor, increased inconvenience, or degraded performance, security administration is an art of balancing risk and cost. A quantitative model for risk assessment is indispensable to make this effort a more scientific process.

Deriving security risk from attack graphs. Since all the attack nodes in an attack graph do not always guarantee success, we can attach a *component metric* to each attack node. The component metric is a numeric measure indicating the conditional probability of attack success when all the preconditions are met. Such component metrics can be derived from CVSS metric vector. For example, we can map the AC metric to probability such that higher AC metric value is mapped to a lower value in probability. Then we can aggregate the probabilities over the attack-graph structure to provide a *cumulative metric*, which indicates the absolute probability of attack success in the specific system. The cumulative metrics are not only affected by the individual vulnerabilities' properties, but are also to a large extent affected by how the security interactions may happen in the specific system which affects the way an attacker can move from one step to another. By combining the component metrics with the attack-graph structure, one can obtain a security metric that is tailored to the specific environment, instead of a generic metric such as the CVSS Base Score.

In the example attack graph of Figure 4, node 7 is attached a component metric 0.2 which is derived from the vulnerability's AC metric based on the mapping High->0.2, Medium-> 0.6, Low -> 0.9. Node 3 has a component metric 1 since it represents network access semantics, not a real attack step and thus without an uncertainty in its success. Since this attack graph is very simple, we can easily see that the cumulative metric for node 8 (compromise of the web server) is also 0.2.

Example 2

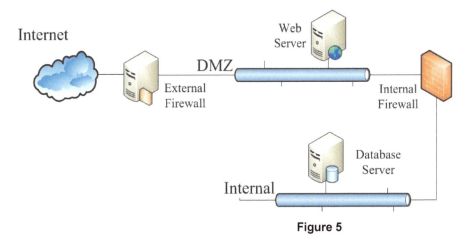

Figure 5

In this example, a new subnet Internal is added, which hosts the database server. The access to the Internal subnet is mediated by an internal firewall. Only the web server can access the database server, which also has a remote vulnerability in the MySQL DB service (CVE-2009-2446). The attack graph for this network is shown in Figure 6.

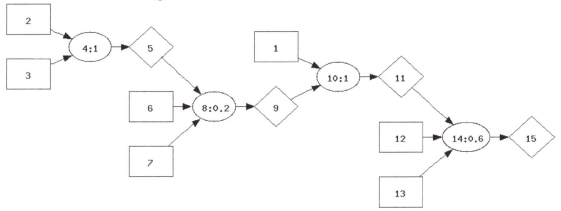

Figure 6

1: hacl(webServer,dbServer,dbProtocol,dbPort)
2: hacl(internet,webServer,httpProtocol,httpPort)
3: attackerLocated(internet)
4: direct network access
5: netAccess(webServer,httpProtocol,httpPort)
6: networkServiceInfo(webServer,httpd,httpProtocol,httpPort,apache)
7: vulExists(webServer,'CVE-2006-3747',httpd,remote,privEscalation)
8: remote exploit of a server program
9: execCode(webServer,apache)
10: multi-hop access
11: netAccess(dbServer,dbProtocol,dbPort)
12: networkServiceInfo(dbServer,mySQL,dbProtocol,dbPort,root)

13: vulExists(dbServer,'CVE-2009-2446',mySQL,remote,privEscalation)
14: remote exploit of a server program
15: execCode(dbServer,root)

This attack graph shows a two-stage attack. The attacker can first compromise the web server (node 8). Then they can use the web server as a stepping stone to further compromise the database server (node 14). The component metric for node 2 is 0.6, since the MySQL vulnerability is easier to exploit than the Apache vulnerability. In this attack graph, since there is only one path to reach the compromise of the database sever (node 15), it is easy to see that the cumulative metric for node 1 is the multiplication of the two component metrics on the path: 0.2x0.6=0.12. This is intuitive since the longer the attack path, the lower the risk.

This example highlights the need to account for security interactions in the specific network to fully understand the risk a vulnerability brings to a system. Although the vulnerability on the database server has a high CVSS score (8.5 in this case), the cumulative risk contributed by the vulnerability to the specific system may be marginal, since it is located at a place hard to get to by an attacker.

Example 3

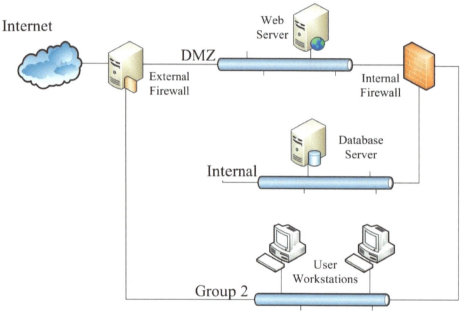

Figure 7

Example 3 adds another subnet to the network, called "Group 2." This subnet contains the user desktop machines used by the company's employees. These machines run the Windows operating system and Internet Explorer (IE) browser. Vulnerability CVE-2009-1918 was identified in IE that would enable execution of arbitrary code on the victim's machine. To exploit this vulnerability, an attacker must trick a user into visiting a maliciously crafted web page. The vulnerability is not a highly complex one to exploit, i.e., once a user visits the malicious page, it is highly likely that their machine will be compromised. The other two vulnerabilities discussed above also exist on the web server and database server in this example. The attack graph for this network is shown in Figure 8.

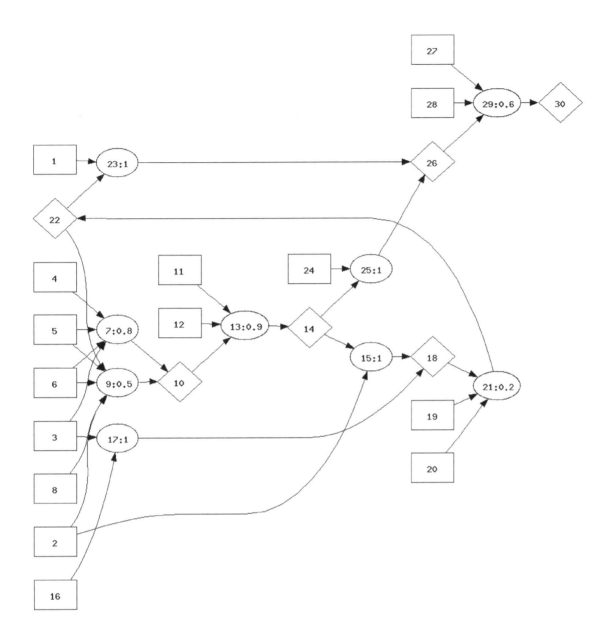

Figure 8

1: hacl(webServer,dbServer,dbProtocol,dbPort)
2: hacl(workStation,webServer,httpProtocol,httpPort)
3: attackerLocated(internet)
4: hacl(workStation,internet,httpProtocol,httpPort)
5: isClient('IE')
6: inCompetent(secretary)
7: Browsing a malicious website
8: isWebServer(webServer)
9: Browsing a compromised website
10: accessMaliciousInput(workStation,secretary,'IE')
11: hasAccount(secretary,workStation,normalAccount)
12: vulExists(workStation,'CVE-2009-1918','IE',remote,privEscalation)

13: remote exploit of a client program
14: execCode(workStation,normalAccount)
15: multi-hop access
16: hacl(internet,webServer,httpProtocol,httpPort)
17: direct network access
18: netAccess(webServer,httpProtocol,httpPort)
19: networkServiceInfo(webServer,httpd,httpProtocol,httpPort,apache)
20: vulExists(webServer,'CVE-2006-3747',httpd,remote,privEscalation)
21: remote exploit of a server program
22: execCode(webServer,apache)
23: multi-hop access
24: hacl(workStation,dbServer,dbProtocol,dbPort)
25: multi-hop access
26: netAccess(dbServer,dbProtocol,dbPort)
27: networkServiceInfo(dbServer,mySQL,dbProtocol,dbPort,root)
28: vulExists(dbServer,'CVE-2009-2446',mySQL,remote,privEscalation)
29: remote exploit of a server program
30: execCode(dbServer,root)

In even such a small network, how security on one machine can affect another can be manifold and non-obvious. A careful examination of the attack graph reveals a number of potential intrusion paths leading to the compromise of the various hosts. An attacker could first compromise the web server and use it as a stepping stone to further attack the database server (3, 17, 18, 21, 22, 23, 26, 29, 30). Or they could first gain control on a user workstation by tricking a user into clicking a malicious link, and launch attacks against the database server from the workstation (3, 7, 10, 13, 14, 25, 26, 29, 30). There are many other attack paths. In general, if we enumerate all possible attack paths in a system, the number could be exponential. However, the privileges and attacks on all these paths are interdependent on each other, and the number of pair-wise inter-dependencies is quadratic to the size of the network. Instead of enumerating all attack paths, a logical attack graph like MulVAL enumerates the interdependencies among the attacks and privileges. This provides an efficient polynomial-time algorithm for computing a compact representation of *all* attack paths in a system.

There are a number of attack nodes in this graph. Nodes 21 and 29 are the exploit against the web server and database server respectively, which have been explained before. An interesting node is 13, which is about the exploit of the IE vulnerability. The component metric 0.9 indicates that this exploit has a high success rate when all the preconditions are met. Of the three preconditions, one of them is that the user (secretary) must access malicious input through the IE program on the host (node 10). This precondition is further calculated by two rules. Node 7 is the instantiation of the following rule:

accessMaliciousInput(H, Victim, Software) :-
    inCompetent(Victim),
    isClient(Software),
    hacl(H, MaliciousMachine, httpProtocol, httpPort),
    attackerLocated(MaliciousMachine).

The predicate "inCompetent" indicates that somebody is not trustworthy for using computers carefully and may fall victim of social-engineering attacks, e.g., clicking a malicious url. The predicate "isClient" indicates that a piece of software is a client software and as a result, the exploit of the vulnerability will need user assistance. This type of information can be obtained from the NVD data as well. Intuitively, the clause specifies that if someone is not careful, and their machine can access a malicious host controlled by an attacker, they may access malicious input provided by the attacker. The component metric assigned to this likelihood is 0.8 as shown in the graph. Basically, this number will need to be provided by the user of the risk analysis tool. Node 9 captures another scenario for the user to access malicious input: they may browse to a compromised web site. This could happen in this network since the attacker could compromise the corporate web server (node 22), and the firewall allows the user workstation to access the corporate web server (node 2). The component metric for node 9 is 0.5, again input by the users. The component metrics like those for nodes 7 and 9 are different from those associated with vulnerabilities. They are affected by the security awareness of users of the enterprise system and are thus context-specific. To provide these metric values, the risk analysis tool can conduct an initial survey asking multiple-choice questions like "How likely will the user of workstations visit a malicious web site?" Based on the answers provided by the system administrator, a set of component metrics representing the above likelihood can be derived and used in subsequent analyses.

It is less obvious how to calculate in this attack graph the likelihood that an attacker can obtain a privilege (e.g., node 30, code-execution privilege on the database server). The complexity comes from shared dependencies and cycles that exist in this attack graph. A number of methods have been developed to handle such complexities and to calculate attack success likelihood in arbitrary attack graphs [25, 34]. We will use this example to illustrate how to use such calculated metrics to aid in security administration.

Using Metrics to Prioritize Risk Mitigation
When considering improvements in network security, a network administrator can be constrained by a variety of factors including money and time. For example, some changes, though preferable, may not be feasible because of the time necessary to make the change and the system downtime that would occur while the change was made. Considering the network topology in Example 3, it is not immediately clear which of the vulnerabilities should be patched first, assuming that a fix is available for each of the three.

Host	Initial scenario	Patch web server	Patch db server	Patch workstations	Change network access
Database server	0.47	0.43	0	0.12	0.12
Web server	0.2	0	0.2	0.2	0.2
Workstations	0.74	0.74	0.74	0	0.74

Table 1: Probabilities of compromise for hosts in Figure 7 (columns reflect different scenarios)

Table 1 shows the metric calculation results based on the method of Homer et al. [34]. Column 2 shows the risk metrics for Example 3. Columns 3-6 show the new risk assessment values based on various mitigation options: patching different vulnerabilities or changing the firewall rules so that the user workstations cannot access the database server. We try to give intuitive reasons to justify the security risk scores for each of the options.

Patching the vulnerability on the web server would eliminate the known risk of compromise for the web server, but would have little effect on the other two hosts. The web server does not contain sensitive information, so protecting this host may not be the best choice. Even if the web server vulnerability gets patched, there are other attack paths. For example, an attacker can first gain control of a user workstation and then launch attacks against the database server from the workstation.

Patching the vulnerability on the database server would eliminate the known risk of compromise for the database server, but have no effect on the risk in the other two hosts, since privileges on the database server do not enable new attacks on the other hosts. This option would secure the sensitive data on the database server, which may be most desirable, but at the cost of having a period of downtime on the database server which may affect business revenues.

Patching the vulnerability on the user workstations would eliminate the risk on itself, as well as significantly reducing the risk in the database server, though the risk in the web server is unchanged. This option secures the workstations and makes the database server more secure, which may be a better solution.

Network configuration changes can also have drastic effects on the security risk. The final column in the table shows the effect of blocking network access from the workstations to the database server. This option eliminates an attack path to the database server that depends on privileges on the workstations, lowering the risk of compromise for the database server, but leaving the web server and workstations vulnerable. Depending on other resource constraints and asset valuations, this may also be a viable solution. There may not be a single "best" option for all organizations. Indeed, different administrators could easily make different choices in this same situation, based on the perceived importance of the hosts and the expected time necessary to carry out a mediation, as well as human resources available. The quantitative risk metrics make clear the effects emerging from each of these possible changes, providing a network administrator with objective data beneficial for judging the relative value of each option.

6. Challenges

There are many challenges for security risk analysis of enterprise networks using attack graphs.

- Enterprise networks can contain hundreds of hosts, with each host running several applications. We need to determine if the current techniques for attack graph generation can scale well for networks containing hundreds of hosts and several applications.
- Obtaining detailed information about exploits is a manual problem. Some of the information about each exploit is available in NVD and CVSS. However, gathering detailed information about an exploit requires human effort that can be large. New techniques are needed to automatically get the exploit information for doing security analysis of enterprise networks.
- Attack graphs for networks with several hosts can contain cycles. These cycles need to be treated properly in security risk analysis. In [25, 34], some preliminary work on how to detect and handle such cycles has been done. Assuming monotonicity in the acquisition of network privileges, such cycles should be excluded in doing the security risk analysis using attack graphs. Handling cycles correctly is a key challenge in this work.
- CVSS scores do not have a fine granularity. Currently the scores are coarse-grained in terms of High, Medium, and Low. A more precise scoring system will improve the overall results of security risk analysis.
- New techniques are needed to model zero-day vulnerabilities about which we have no prior knowledge or experience. New techniques need to be developed for security risk analysis of networks against potential zero-day attacks. We have some preliminary results on modeling zero day attacks [35].

7. Conclusions

This report explores an approach to solve the system administrator's problem of how to analyze the security risk of enterprise networks. It also shows how to select security hardening measures from a given set of security mechanisms so as to minimize the risk to enterprise systems from network attacks.

We have presented a model and a methodology for security risk analysis of enterprise networks using probabilistic attack graphs. This model annotates the attack graph with known vulnerabilities and their likelihoods of exploitation. By propagating the exploit likelihoods through the attack graph, a metric is computed that quantifies the overall security risk of enterprise networks. This methodology can be applied to evaluate and improve the security risk of enterprise systems. The experiments discussed in this report show the effectiveness of our approach and how it can be used by the system administrators to decide among the different risk mitigation options.

8. References

1. A. Jaquith, *Security Metrics: Replacing Fear, Uncertainty, and Doubt*, Addison Wesley, 2007.
2. L. Wang, A. Singhal, S. Jajodia, "Measuring the Overall Security of Network Configurations using Attack Graphs," in *Proceedings of the 21st IFIP WG 11.3 Working Conference on Data and Applications Security*, Springer-Verlag, 2007.
3. J. Pamula, S. Jajodia, P. Ammann, V. Swarup, "A Weakest-Adversary Security Metric for Network Configuration Security Analysis," in *Proceedings of the 2nd ACM Workshop on Quality of Protection*, ACM Press, 2006.
4. "The Systems Security Engineering Capability Maturity Model," http://www.sse-cmm.org/index.html.
5. M. Swanson, N. Bartol, J. Sabato, J Hash, L. Graffo, *Security Metrics Guide for Information Technology Systems*, Special Publication 800-55, National Institute of Standards and Technology, July 2003.
6. G. Stoneburner, C. Hayden, A Feringa, *Engineering Principles for Information Technology Security*, Special Publication 800-27 (Rev A), National Institute of Standards and Technology, June 2004.
7. P. Mell, K. Scarforne and S. Romanosky, "A Complete Guide to the Common Vulnerability Scoring System (CVSS) Version 2.0," http://www.first.org/cvss/cvss-guide.html.
8. R. Ritchey, P. Ammann, "Using Model Checking to Analyze Network Vulnerabilities," in *Proceedings of the IEEE Symposium on Security and Privacy*, 2000.
9. O. Sheyner, J. Haines, S. Jha, R. Lippmann, J. Wing, "Automated Generation and Analysis of Attack Graphs," in *Proceedings of the IEEE Symposium on Security and Privacy*, 2002.
10. P. Ammann, D. Wijesekera, S. Kaushik, "Scalable, Graph-Based Network Vulnerability Analysis," in *Proceedings of the ACM Conference on Computer and Communications Security*, 2002.
11. R. Lippmann, K. Ingols, C. Scott, K. Piwowarski, K. Kratkiewicz, M. Artz, R. Cunningham, "Validating and Restoring Defense in Depth Using Attack Graphs," MILCOM Military Communications Conference, 2006.
12. S. Noel, J. Jajodia, "Understanding Complex Network Attack Graphs through Clustered Adjacency Matrices," in *Proceedings of the 21st Annual Computer Security Applications Conference*, 2005.
13. S. Noel, S. Jajodia, "Managing Attack Graph Complexity through Visual Hierarchical Aggregation," in *Proceedings of the ACM CCS Workshop on Visualization and Data Mining for Computer Security*, 2004.
14. S. Noel, S. Jajodia, "Advanced Vulnerability Analysis and Intrusion Detection through Predictive Attack Graphs," Critical Issues in C4I, Armed Forces Communications and Electronics Association (AFCEA) Solutions Series, 2009.
15. S. Noel, S. Jajodia, "Proactive Intrusion Prevention and Response via Attack Graphs," in *Practical Intrusion Detection*, Ryan Trost (ed.), Addison-Wesley Professional, in preparation.
16. F. Cuppens, R. Ortalo, "LAMBDA: A Language to Model a Database for Detection of Attacks," in *Proceedings of the Workshop on Recent Advances in Intrusion Detection*, 2000.

17. S. Templeton, K. Levitt, "A Requires/Provides Model for Computer Attacks," in *Proceedings of the New Security Paradigms Workshop*, 2000.

18. R. Ritchey, B. O'Berry, S. Noel, "Representing TCP/IP Connectivity for Topological Analysis of Network Security," in *Proceedings of the 18th Annual Computer Security Applications Conference*, 2002.

19. Skybox Security, http://www.skyboxsecurity.com/.

20. RedSeal Systems, http://www.redseal.net/.

21. R. Lippmann, K. Ingols, "An Annotated Review of Past Papers on Attack Graphs," Lincoln Laboratory Technical Report ESC-TR-2005-054, 2005.

22. S. Jajodia, S. Noel, B. O'Berry, "Topological Analysis of Network Attack Vulnerability," in *Managing Cyber Threats: Issues, Approaches and Challenges*, V. Kumar, J. Srivastava, A. Lazarevic (eds.), Springer, 2005.

23. Nessus Vulnerability Scanner, http://www.nessus.org.

24. Retina Security Scanner, http://www.eeye.com/..

25. L. Wang, T. Islam, T. Long, A. Singhal and S. Jajodia, "An Attack Graph Based Probabilistic Security Metrics," Proceedings of 22nd IFIP WG 11.3 Working Conference on Data and Application Security (DBSEC 2008), London, UK, July 2008.

26. A. Singhal and S. Xou, "Techniques for Enterprise Network Security Metrics," Proceedings of 2009 Cyber Security and Information Intelligence Research Workshop, Oakridge National Labs, Oakridge, April 2009.

27. M. Frigault, L. Wang, A. Singhal and S. Jajodia, "Measuring Network Security Using Dynamic Bayesian Network," 2008 ACM Workshop on Quality of Protection, October 2008.

28. P. Manadhata, J. Wing, M. Flynn and M. McQueen. "Measuring the attack surface of two FTP daemons," Proceedings of 2nd ACM Workshop on Quality of Protection, 2006.

29. K. Ingols, R. Lippmann and K. Piwowarski, "Practical Attack Graph Generation for Network Defense," Proceedings of ACSAC Conference 2006.

30. K. Ingols, M. Chu, R. Lippmann, S. Webster and S. Boyer, "Modeling Modern Network Attacks and Countermeasures Using Attack Graphs," Proceedings of ACSAC Conference 2009.

31. X. Ou, W.F. Boyer and M.A. McQueen. "A Scalable Approach to Attack Graph Generation," Proceedings of 13th ACM CCS Conference, pages 336-345, 2006.

32. X. Ou, S. Govindavajhala, and A. W. Apple, "MULVAL: A logic based network security analyzer," 14th USENIX Security Symposium, 2005.

33. P. Manadhata, J. Wing, M. Flynn and M. McQuen, "Measuring the attack surfaces of two FTP daemons," Proceedings of the 2nd ACM Workshop on Quality of Protection, 2006.

34. J. Homer, X. Ou, and D. Schmidt. "A sound and practical approach to quantifying security risk in enterprise networks," Technical report, Kansas State University, Computing and Information Sciences Department, August 2009.

35. Wang, Jajodia, Singhal, Noel, "K Zero Day Safety: Measuring the Security of Networks against Unknown Attacks," European Symposium on Research in Computer Security (ESORICS) September 2010.

36. Stoneburner G., Goguen A., Feringa A., NIST Special Publication 800-30, Risk Management Guide for Information Technology Systems, March 2001.

37. Chew E., Swanson M., Stine K. Bartol N., Brown A., and Robinson W., NIST Special Publication 800-55 Revision 1, Performance Measurement Guide for Information Security," July 2008.

38. Joint Task Force Transformation Initiative, NIST Special Publication 800-39, Managing Information Security Risk, Organization, Mission and Information System Review, March 2011.